HELF

GUIDELINES IN ...NG

PEOPLE'S
HARM

AUTHORED BY : IBN TAYMIYYAH

EXPLANATORY NOTES BY:
SHAYKH 'ABDUR-RAZZAQ IBN 'ABDUL-MUHSIN AL-'ABBAD
AL-BADR

ISBN: 978-1-9442-4869-7

First Edition: Rabī' Awwal 1437 A.H. / January 2016 C.E.

Cover Design: Abū Sulaymān Muhammad 'Abdul-Azim Ibn Joshua Baker

Translation by: Abū Sulaymān Muhammad 'Abdul-Azim Ibn Joshua Baker

Revision of translation by Abdullah Ibrāhīm Omrān
abdullahomran44@live.com

Editing by Maktabatulirshad staff

Typesetting & formatting by Abū Sulaymān Muhammad "Abdul-Azim Ibn Joshua Baker

Printing: Ohio Printing

Subject: Akhlāq

Website: www.maktabatulirshad.com
E-mail: info@maktabatulirshad.com

Table of Contents

BRIEF BIOGRAPHY OF THE AUTHOR

His name: Shaykh 'Abdur-Razzāq Ibn 'Abdul-Muhsin al-'Abbād al-Badr.

He is the son of the *'Allāmah* and *Muhaddith* of Medina Shaykh 'Abdul-Muhsin al 'Abbād al-Badr.

Birth: He was born on the 22nd day of *Dhul-Qa'dah* in the year 1382 AH in az-Zal'fi, Kingdom of Saudi Arabia. He currently resides in Medina.

Current Occupation: He is a member of the teaching staff at the Islāmic University of Medina.

Scholastic Certifications: Doctorate in *'Aqīdah*.

The Shaykh has authored books, researches, as well as numerous explanations in different disciplines. Among them are:

1. *Fiqh of Supplications & adh-Kār.*

2. *Hajj & Refinement of Souls.*

3. Explanation of 'Exemplary Principles' by Shaykh Ibn 'Uthaymīn (رَحِمَهُ ٱللَّهُ).

4. Explanation of the book, The Principles of Names & Attributes, authored by Shaykh-ul-Islām Ibn al-Qayyim (رَحِمَهُ ٱللَّهُ).

5. Explanation of the book, Good Words, authored by Shaykh-ul-Islām Ibn al-Qayyim (رَحِمَهُ ٱللَّهُ).

6. Explanation of the book, al-Aqīdah at-Tahāwiyyah.

7. Explanation of the book, Fusūl: Biography of the Messenger, by Ibn Kathīr (رَحِمَهُ ٱللَّهُ).

8. An explanation of the book, al-Adab-ul-Mufrad, authored by Imam Bukhārī (رَحِمَهُ ٱللَّهُ).

From the most distinguished scholars whom he has learned knowledge from are:

1. His father the 'Allāmah Shaykh 'Abdul-Muhsin al-Badr (حَفِظَهُ الله).

2. The 'Allāmah Shaykh Ibn Bāz (رَحِمَهُ ٱللَّهُ).

3. The 'Allāmah Shaykh Muhammad Ibn Sālih al-'Uthaymīn (رَحِمَهُ ٱللَّهُ).

4. Shaykh 'Ali Ibn Nāsir al-Faqīhi (حَفِظَهُ الله).

ARABIC SYMBOL TABLE

Arabic Symbols & their meanings

حفظه الله	May Allāh preserve him
رَضِيَ ٱللَّهُ عَنْهُ	(i.e. a male companion of the Prophet Muhammad)
سُبْحَانَهُ وَتَعَالَى	Glorified & Exalted is Allāh
عَزَّوَجَلَّ	(Allāh) the Mighty & Sublime
تَبَارَكَ وَتَعَالَى	(Allāh) the Blessed & Exalted
جَلَّ وَعَلَا	(Allāh) the Sublime & Exalted
عَلَيْهِ ٱلصَّلَاةُ وَٱلسَّلَامُ	May Allāh send Blessings & Safety upon him (i.e. a Prophet or Messenger)
صَلَّى ٱللَّهُ عَلَيْهِ وَعَلَى آلِهِ وَسَلَّمَ	May Allāh send Blessings & Safety upon him and his family (i.e. Du'ā sent when mentioning the Prophet Muhammad)
رَحِمَهُ ٱللَّهُ	May Allāh have mercy upon him
رَضِيَ ٱللَّهُ عَنْهُمْ	May Allāh be pleased with them (i.e. Du'ā made for the Companions of the Prophet Muhammad)
جَلَّ جَلَالُهُ	(Allāh) His Majesty is Exalted
رَضِيَ ٱللَّهُ عَنْهَا	رَضِيَ ٱللَّهُ عَنْهَا (i.e. a female companion of the Prophet Muhammad)

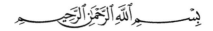

INTRODUCTION

All praise belongs to Allāh, the Lord of all that exists; I testify that none has the right to be worshiped in truth except Allāh Alone, Who has no partners, and I testify that Muhammad is His servant and Messenger. May Allāh grant peace to him, his family, and all of His companions and grant them the highest rank.

O Allāh grant our souls Taqwā and purify our souls. Indeed, You are the best for purifying it. You are its Protector and Master.

O Allāh guide us to the best of morals and etiquettes; no one can guide us to them except You. Please turn bad morals away from us; no one can do so except You (alone).

To proceed:

Indeed, patience is one of the greatest statuses in the religion and occupies one of its loftiest classes. Allāh (سُبْحَانَهُ وَتَعَالَى) mentions it in numerous places throughout His Book (جَلَّ وَعَلَا). Imām Ahmad (رَحِمَهُ ٱللَّهُ) said about it,

"Allāh mentions patience in the Noble Qur'ān more than ninety times."[1]

This statement (of Imām Ahmad) shows in a clear fashion the great and prestigious status of Patience; also, to the servants' dire need to practice it in both performing acts of obedience and abandoning acts of disobedience; patience is also required during destined trials to avoid impatience and displeasure. The servant is in need of patience. Patience accompanies the Muslim in all of his circumstances; it is essential in performing acts of obedience, avoiding acts of disobedience, and receiving trials with what pleases Allāh.

So how much in need is the Muslim (of this)! Rather, he is in more severe need to adorn himself with patience in all of his circumstances!

Allāh (سُبْحَانَهُ وَتَعَالَى) mentions Patience in numerous places throughout the Qur'ān. It comes in the form of a command; it comes in the form of a prohibition (i.e., impatience); It comes in the form of a praise to those who have it. The Qur'ān mentions what Allāh (سُبْحَانَهُ وَتَعَالَى) has prepared for them of an abundant reward and beautiful abode. Unlimited glad tidings

---

[1] Refer to the book *Madārij as-Sālikīn* by ibn ul-Qayyim (1/130); published by *Dār ul-Kitāb al-Arabī* in Beirut.

INTRODUCTION

are promised to those who have patience. Allāh
(سُبْحَانَهُوَتَعَالَى) informs (us) that He loves them, and that He
gives them aid, support, and protection; Patience is
mentioned in different shapes/forms elsewhere in the
Book of Allāh (سُبْحَانَهُوَتَعَالَى).

All of this attest to the great status of Patience; its lofty
station, and (our) urgent need for it.

The discussion on Patience is an elaborate one,
reaching numerous areas and multiple views. So our
discussion will be limited to a particular sub-topic
related to it. It is:

"Enduring people's harm."

What is well-known is that one is not safe from the
harms of people in this life because people are of
(various) types, different in their morals, origins,
natural dispositions, and interactions. So it is necessary
for the Muslim to adorn himself with patience.

From the (various forms) of patience necessary for the
Muslim to adorn himself with is enduring the people's
harm which is an area that many ambitions and desires
attempted to achieve however fell short of obtaining it.
For this reason, the statements of the people of
knowledge expounding on what aids the person to

endure the harm of people is considered to be like a lamp and source of light for the Muslim in this area.

This topic that we will tackle using explanatory notes is the abbreviated speech from one of Shaykh-ul Islām Ibn Taymīyah's (رَحِمَهُ ٱللَّهُ) treatises that discusses Patience.

May Allāh have mercy on this Imām, and how beautiful was his series of advice and how excellent was his clarifications! May Allāh reward him (رَحِمَهُ ٱللَّهُ) for his efforts and give him a complete reward; May Allāh grant him the highest station in paradise — indeed Allāh (سُبْحَانَهُ وَتَعَالَى) is All-hearing, Near, and answers the (supplication).

I ask Allāh, the Generous, Who has facilitated for us, this explanatory notes on Shaykh-ul Islām Ibn Taymīyah's (رَحِمَهُ ٱللَّهُ) speech concerning what is mentioned about what will aid in enduring people's harm. May Allāh make that a source of aid for all of us towards this type of Patience. May He make us among His patience and grateful servants because the religion is of two halves: Patience and Gratitude. For this reason, it has been stated, **"Patience is half of the religion."**

INTRODUCTION

We ask Allāh, the Generous, to benefit us by what He has taught us; May He increase us in knowledge; and May He make what we learn a proof for us and not against us. Indeed, He (تَبَارَكَوَتَعَالَى) is All-Hearing, Near, and answers (the supplication).

THE FIRST MATTER

Shaykh-ul Islām Taymīyah (رَحِمَهُ ٱللَّهُ) said,

وَ يُعِينُ الْعَبْدَ عَلَى هَذَا الصَّبْرِ عِدَّةُ أَشْيَاءَ :

أَحَدُهَا : أَنْ يَشْهَدَ أَنَّ اللهَ سُبْحَانَهُ وَ تَعَالَى خَالِقُ

أَفْعَالِ الْعِبَادِ؛ حَرَكَاتِهِمْ وَ سَكَنَاتِهِمْ وَ إِرَادَتِهِمْ

، فَمَا شَاءَ اللهُ كَانَ وَ مَا لَمْ يَشَأْ لَمْ يَكُنْ ، فَلَا

يَتَحَرَّكُ فِي الْعَالَمِ الْعُلْوِيِّ وَ السُّفْلِيِّ ذَرَّةٌ إِلَّا

بِإِذْنِهِ وَ مَشِيئَتِهِ، فَالْعِبَادُ آلَةٌ، فَانْظُرْ إِلَى الَّذِي

سَلَّطَهُمْ عَلَيْكَ وَ لَا تَنْظُرْ إِلَى فِعْلِهِمْ بِكَ ،

تَسْتَرِحْ مِنَ الْهَمِّ وَ الْغَمِّ .

"A number of things will aid the servant with this (type) of Patience.

The first of them is that one attests that Allāh (سُبْحَانَهُ وَتَعَالَى) is the Creator of the servants' actions; as well as their movements (in all of their doings), their wants. So whatever Allāh wills comes into existence and whatever He did not want cannot come into existence. Not even an atom's weight will move in the upper and lower part of the universe except by His permission and Supreme will. The servants are under Allāh's subjugation—so turn your attention to the One, who empowered them, and do not turn your attention to their actions against you. You will be relieved of grief and anxiety."

Explanatory Notes

This statement is the first matter that He (i.e. the author) (رَحِمَهُ ٱللَّهُ) began to mention about the matters that aid in having patience. The servant should attest to the creation of the servants' actions, and that the servants' actions have been created and the servant cannot will any matter pertaining to actions unless Allāh had will it (first) as stated:

$$ \text{﴿ وَمَا تَشَاءُونَ إِلَّا أَن يَشَاءَ ٱللَّهُ رَبُّ ٱلْعَالَمِينَ ۝ ﴾} $$

"And you will not, unless (it be) that Allāh wills, the Lord of the 'Alamin (mankind, jinns and all that exists)." [Sūrah at-Takwīr 81:29]

So when you bear in mind that not a single movement or any matter of the servants are not done except by the Divine decree and ordainment of Allāh (سُبْحَانَهُوَتَعَالَى); and that all of their actions or any of their movements have been decreed by Allāh (سُبْحَانَهُوَتَعَالَى). So turn your attention to this matter from this angle (direction). Also, that Allāh (سُبْحَانَهُوَتَعَالَى) has given these individuals power to harm him, and what necessitated it? What caused it on part of the servant's actions?

You should turn your attention to the fact that these individuals' actions are only from what Allāh decreed, and all of the servants' actions were created by Allāh (سُبْحَانَهُوَتَعَالَى); thus your attention should be in this direction. Look towards the One, who gave them the power over you and don't look to their actions.

When you look towards who gave them the power to cause you harm you will begin to recognize the causes that led to such empowerment (over you). This matter will be clarified by the author (رَحِمَهُٱللَّهُ) later.

THE SECOND MATTER

Shaykh-ul Islām ibn Taymīyah (رَحِمَهُٱللَّهُ) said,

الثَّانِي – مِمَّا يُعِينُ الْعَبْدَ عَلَى هَذَا الصَّبْرِ – :
أَنْ يَشْهَدَ ذُنُوبَهُ، وَ أَنَّ اللهَ إِنَّمَا سَلَّطَهُمْ عَلَيْهِ
بِذَنْبِهِ، كَمَا قَالَ تَعَالَى : ﴿ وَمَآ أَصَٰبَكُم مِّن مُّصِيبَةٍ
فَبِمَا كَسَبَتْ أَيْدِيكُمْ وَيَعْفُواْ عَن كَثِيرٍ ﴿٣٠﴾ ﴾

فَإِذَا شَهِدَ الْعَبْدُ أَنْ جَمِيعَ مَا يَنَالُهُ مِنَ الْمَكْرُوهِ
فَسَبَبُهُ ذُنُوبُهُ؛ اشْتَغَلَ بِالتَّوْبَةِ وَ الْاسْتِغْفَارِ مِنَ
الذُّنُوبِ الَّتِي سَلَّطَهُمْ عَلَيْهِ بِسَبَبِهَا عَنْ ذَمِّهِمْ
وَ لَوْمِهِمْ وَالْوَقِيعَةِ فِيهِمْ.

وَ إِذَا رَأَيْتَ الْعَبْدَ يَقَعُ فِي النَّاسِ إِذَا آذَوْهُ وَ لَا يَرْجِعُ
إِلَى نَفْسِهِ بِاللَّوْمِ وَ الْاسْتِغْفَارِ؛ فَاعْلَمْ أَنَّ
مُصِيبَتَهُ مُصِيبَةٌ حَقِيقِيَّةٌ.

وَ إِذَا تَابَ وَاسْتَغْفَرَ وَ قَالَ : ((هَـذَا بِـذُنُـوبِي)) ؛

صَارَتْ فِي حَقِّهِ نِعْمَةً .

قَالَ عَلِيُّ بْنِ أَبِي طَالِبٍ رَضِيَ اللهُ عَنْهُ كَلِمَةً مِنْ

جَوَاهِرِ الْكَلَام : لَا يَرْجُوَنَّ عَبْدٌ إِلَّا رَبَّهُ ، وَ لَا

يَخَافَنَّ عَبْدٌ إِلَّا ذَنْبَهُ . وَ رُوِيَ عَنْهُ وَ عَنْ غَيْرِهِ :

مَا نُزِلَ بَلَاءٌ إِلَّا بِذَنْبٍ ، وَ لَا رُفِعَ إِلَّا بِتَوْبَةٍ .

"The second (matter) is that one should recognize his sins and that Allāh only gave them power over him because of his sins just as He (سُبْحَانَهُ وَتَعَالَى) says,

"And whatever of misfortune befalls you, it is because of what your hands have earned. And He pardons much." [Sūrah ash-Shura 42:30]

So when the servant has recognized that all of what he goes through of disliked matters resulted because of his sins, he should occupy himself with repenting and seeking forgiveness for the sins that, because of it, Allāh gave the people power to blame, censure, and disparage him.

When you see the servant (person) disparaging the people when they harm him instead of blaming himself, and he doesn't seek forgiveness then know that his calamity is serious.

On the other hand, if you see him repenting and seeking forgiveness saying, 'this (harm) is because of my sins' then this calamity becomes a blessing for him.

'Ali ibn Abī Tālib (رضي الله عنه) said a statement from the gems of speech, 'Indeed a servant should hope in Allāh exclusively and should not dread anything except his sins.' He and others also reported it, 'Not a single calamity descends except because of a sin and will not be lifted except by repenting.'"

Explanatory notes

This second matter is among the matters that will aid with enduring people's harm; it is built on what was previously (mentioned). So when the servant contemplates that the servants' actions are created, and he looks, on this occasion, to Who gave the servants power to harm (him), he will refer blame and reproof upon himself saying, 'Allāh only gave these individuals power to harm me because of my sins, negligence, and abandonment.' So in exchange for busying himself with insulting, disparaging, and blaming them he occupies himself with faulting himself; and that his sins necessitate these people to have the power to harm him. So he increases seeking forgiveness and repenting to Allāh (سُبْحَانَهُوَتَعَالَى) from these sins which he knows about or is ignorant of — thus he repents to Allāh and increases in seeking forgiveness.

In this way, Shaykh-ul Islām Ibn Taymīyah (رَحِمَهُٱللَّهُ) transmitted this precious statement of 'Ali ibn Abī Tālib (رَضِيَٱللَّهُعَنْهُ) that is actualized in which he said,

لَا يَـرْجُـوَنَّ عَـبْدٌ إِلَّا رَبَّـهُ، وَ لَا يَـخَـافَـنَّ عَـبْدٌ إِلَّا ذَنْبَـهُ

"Indeed, a servant should hope in Allāh exclusively and should not dread anything except his sins."

So the statement, **"a servant should hope in Allāh exclusively"** regarding all of his needs, and religious and worldly requests because all matters are in the hands of Allāh (سُبْحَانَهُوَتَعَالَى).

THE SECOND MATTER

And the statement, **"one should not dread anything except his sins"** because his sins bring about his own destruction and ruin. Thus, not a single calamity descends except because of a sin and it will not be lifted except by repenting.

THE THIRD MATTER

Shaykh-ul Islām Ibn Taymīyah (رَحِمَهُٱللَّهُ) said,

الثَّالِثُ : أَنْ يَشْهَدَ الْعَبْدُ حُسْنَ الثَّوَابِ الَّذِي وَعَدَهُ اللهُ لِمَنْ عَفَا وَ صَبَرَ، كَمَا قَالَ تَعَالَى : ﴿ وَجَزَٰٓؤُاْ سَيِّئَةٖ سَيِّئَةٞ مِّثْلُهَاۖ فَمَنْ عَفَا وَأَصْلَحَ فَأَجْرُهُۥ عَلَى ٱللَّهِۚ إِنَّهُۥ لَا يُحِبُّ ٱلظَّٰلِمِينَ ﴾ ٤٠

وَ لَمَّا كَانَ النَّاسُ عِنْدَ مُقَابَلَةِ الْأَذَى ثَلَاثَةُ أَقْسَامٍ : ظَالِمٌ يَأْخُذُ فَوْقَ حَقِّهِ، وَ مُقْتَصِدٌ يَأْخُذُ بِقَدَرِ حَقِّهِ، وَ مُحْسِنٌ يَعْفُو وَ يَتْرُكُ حَقَّهُ، ذَكَرَ الْأَقْسَامَ الثَّلَاثَةَ فِي هَذِهِ الْآيَةِ، فَأَوَّلُهَا لِلْمُقْتَصِدِينَ، وَ وَسَطُهَا لِلسَّابِقِينَ، وَ آخِرُهَا لِلظَّالِمِينَ .

وَ يَشْهَدُ نِدَاءَ الْمُنَادِي يَوْمَ الْقِيَامَةِ : ((أَ لَا لِيَقُمْ مَنْ وَجَبَ أَجْرُهُ عَلَى اللهِ)) ، فَلَا يَقُمْ إِلَّا مَنْ عَفَا

وَ أَصْلَحَ ، وَ إِذَا شَهِدَ مَعَ ذَلِكَ فُوتَ الْأَجْرُ
بِالْإِنْتِقَامِ وَ الْإِسْتِيفَاءِ سَهُلَ عَلَيْهِ الصَّبْرُ وَ
الْعَفْوُ.

"The Third matter is that the servant recognizes the splendid reward that Allāh has promised for the one who lets (others) go unpunished and has patience (i.e., against harm) just as Allāh (سُبْحَانَهُوَتَعَالَى) says,

"The recompense for an evil is an evil like thereof, but whoever forgives and makes reconciliation, his reward is due from Allāh. Verily, He likes not the Zālimūn (oppressors, polytheists, and wrong-doers, etc.)." [Sūrah ash-Shura' 42:40]

As for when people encounter harm they are of three categories:

1. The one who oppresses that takes more than his right.

2. The moderate person who takes his due right.

3. Muhsin, who pardons and leaves taking (back) his right.

These three categories are cited in this verse. The first of them are those who take a middle course, the second, as mentioned in the verse, are those who are foremost in deeds, and the last of them mentioned are those who are oppressors.

One will attest to the one who announces on the day of Resurrection saying, 'The one whom Allāh promised to reward shall rise.' At this point, the specified person and none but him shall rise. Moreover, if the person recognizes (the fact) that the reward is to be missed if he were to seek revenge, then patience and forgiveness would be easy to embrace."

Explanatory notes

This (previous mentioned statement) is the third **'matter that the servant recognizes the splendid reward'** meaning what Allāh (سُبْحَانَهُوَتَعَالَ) has prepared for those who forbear people's harm and pardon them.

These two categories, one of which is better than the other. The first category is patience in the face of people's harm, and the higher of the two is pardoning them. Pardoning, of course, is the loftier status,

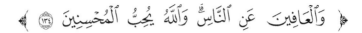

﴿ وَٱلْعَافِينَ عَنِ ٱلنَّاسِ وَٱللَّهُ يُحِبُّ ٱلْمُحْسِنِينَ ۝ ﴾

"and who pardon men; verily, Allāh loves Al-Muhsinūn (the good-doers)." [*Sūrah Ali Imrān 3:134*]

So this is a status of showing goodness to others; and not every person can reach this level. Rather, the only one from Allāh's servants (تَبَارَكَوَتَعَالَى) who will reach this level is he who is close to Allāh and worship Allāh upon Ihsān. So for that to be obtained, he must recognize the reward and good recompense. So he becomes patient upon their harm aspiring for what is with Allāh of (the) good recompense, or he should aim for the higher reward, which is pardoning those who harmed him in order to gain Allāh's reward; for indeed Allāh's loves those who pardon people.

The author (رَحِمَهُٱللَّهُ) cites this noble verse:

﴿ وَجَزَٰٓؤُاْ سَيِّئَةٍ سَيِّئَةٌ مِّثْلُهَا فَمَنْ عَفَا وَأَصْلَحَ فَأَجْرُهُ عَلَى ٱللَّهِ إِنَّهُ لَا يُحِبُّ ٱلظَّٰلِمِينَ ۝ ﴾

"The recompense for an evil is an evil like thereof, but whoever forgives and makes reconciliation, his reward is due from Allāh. Verily, He likes not the Zālimūn (oppressors, polytheists, and wrong-doers, etc.)." [*Sūrah ash-Shura* 42:40]

Allāh (سُبْحَانَهُوَتَعَالَى) mentions within this verse three classes pertaining to peoples' circumstances when they are tried (suffer) from the harm of people:

The first class: is repaying bad with bad similar to it, and punishing the transgressor with the same without exceeding the bounds. This matter is permissible as mentioned in the verse,

$$﴿ وَجَزَٰٓؤُاْ سَيِّئَةٍ سَيِّئَةٌ مِّثْلُهَا ﴾$$

"The recompense for an evil is an evil like thereof."

and similarly in another verse Allāh (سُبْحَانَهُوَتَعَالَى) says,

$$﴿ وَإِنْ عَاقَبْتُمْ فَعَاقِبُواْ بِمِثْلِ مَا عُوقِبْتُم بِهِۦ وَلَئِن صَبَرْتُمْ لَهُوَ خَيْرٌ لِّلصَّٰبِرِينَ ۝ ﴾$$

"And if you punish (your enemy, O you believers in the Oneness of Allāh), then punish them with the like of that with which you were afflicted. But if you endure patiently, verily, it is better for *As-Sābirīn* (the patient ones, etc.)." [*Sūrah an-Nahl* 16:126]

The second class: it is pardoning which is the highest level. For this reason, Allāh (سُبْحَانَهُوَتَعَالَى) says,

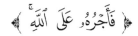

"but whoever forgives and makes reconciliation, his reward is due from Allāh."

Its giver measures the (value) of a reward, and in this case, Allāh is the giver. He says (سُبْحَانَهُوَتَعَالَى),

$$ ﴾ فَأَجْرُهُ عَلَى ٱللَّهِ ﴿ $$

"his reward is due from Allāh."

Meaning, the reward of these individuals and their compensation is great and abundant from Allāh (سُبْحَانَهُوَتَعَالَى).

The third class: Which is punishing in the most severe way; transgressing and exceeding the bounds, and this is an act of oppression. Allāh (سُبْحَانَهُوَتَعَالَى) mentioned this class in His statement,

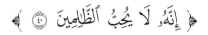

"Verily, He likes not the Zālimūn (oppressors, polytheists, and wrong-doers, etc.)."

Hence, people are divided into three types under this class.

1. The wrongdoer who takes more than his right.

2. The one who takes the middle course where he only takes his right.

3. The Muhsin who pardons and foregoes his right, which is the best of all the types.

Allāh listed these categories within this noble verse. Shaykh-ul Islām Ibn Taymīyah (رَحِمَهُ ٱللَّه) then said, "**And the servant recognizes**" — meaning of the splendid reward. When the call for those who are promised Allāh's reward is announced; whereby those referred to shall rise, as narrated in the completion of the Hadīth. That Hadīth's chain of narration is questionable, however, the earlier verse is enough on its own because Allāh (سُبْحَانَهُ وَتَعَالَى) says,

$$\text{﴾ فَمَنْ عَفَا وَأَصْلَحَ فَأَجْرُهُ عَلَى ٱللَّهِ ﴿}$$

"**but whoever forgives and makes reconciliation, his reward is due from Allāh.**"

THE FOURTH MATTER

Shaykh-ul Islām Ibn Taymīyah (رَحِمَهُ ٱللَّهُ) said,

الـرَّابِعُ : أَنْ يَشْهَدَ أَنَّهُ إِذَا عَفَا وَ أَحْسَنَ ، أَوْرَثَهُ ذَلِكَ
مِنْ سَلَامَةِ الْقَلْبِ لِإِخْوَانِهِ وَ نَقَائِهِ مِنَ الْغِشِّ وَ
الْغِلِّ وَ طَلَبِ الْإِنْتِقَامِ وَإِرَادَةِ الشَّرِّ ، وَ حَصَلَ لَهُ
مِنْ حَلَاوَةِ الْعَفْوِ مَا يَزِيدُ لَذَّتَهُ وَ مَنْفَعَتَهُ عَاجِلاً
وَ آجِلًا عَلَى الْمَنْفَعَةِ الْحَاصِلَةِ لَهُ بِالْإِنْتِقَامِ
أَضْعَافاً مُضَاعَفَةً ، وَ يَدْخُلُ فِي قَوْلِهِ تَعَالَى : ،
فَيَصِيرُ مَحْبُوبًا لله، وَ يَصِيرُ حَالُهُ حَالَ مَنْ أُخِذَ
مِنْهُ دِرْهَمٌ فَعُوضَ عَلَيْهِ أُلُوفًا مِنَ الدَّنَانِيرِ ،
فَحِينَئِذٍ يَفْرَحُ بِمَا مَنَّ اللهُ عَلَيْهِ أَعْظَمَ فَرَحًا
يَكُونُ.

"The fourth matter is that one recognizes when he pardons and treats others good, he shall be rewarded with a peaceful heart towards his brothers and his heart will be unstained by swindling, spite, seeking revenge, or desiring evil.

He will obtain the sweetness of pardoning that exceeds his delight and benefit worldly and in the hereafter more than the benefit achieved by revenge many times over. This falls under Allāh's statement (سُبْحَانَهُۥوَتَعَالَ),

"Allāh loves *Al-Muhsinūn* (the good-doers)." [*Sūrah Ali Imran* 3:134]

As a result, he will become beloved by Allāh, and he would be similar to the person whose Dirham was taken but to be replaced with thousands of Dinārs. So at that moment, he shall rejoice indescribably due to what Allāh has bestowed upon him."

Explanatory notes

Meaning, that if one were to pardon and treat others with excellence, then he will inherit from that a peaceful heart towards his brothers and his heart will be unstained by swindling, seeking revenge, and desiring evil.

THE FOURTH MATTER

Some people seek revenge in order to satisfy their thirst for revenge and to be pleased assuming that by revenge they will feel ease; however, the matter is the exact opposite as the author (رَحِمَهُ ٱللَّهُ) explained. Ease is achieved in pardoning; the person's ease and delight in this area are in pardoning. Pardoning increases the servant in honor.

Some might think that letting someone go unpunished is a form of humiliation! Yet it only increases him in honor, ease, joy, and a friendly atmosphere. He should realize this fact because when he pardons he becomes pleased and his chest is unimpaired by spite, hatred, and envy; rather he pardons, seeks what is with Allāh (i.e., a reward) and his heart will be at ease. This matter has a tremendous status if the servant is granted success to experience it, and by Allāh's permission (تَبَارَكَ وَتَعَالَىٰ) he will be aided by having patience with people's harm.

THE FIFTH MATTER

Shaykh-ul Islām Ibn Taymīyah (رَحِمَهُٱللَّهُ) said,

الْـخَـامِـسُ : أَنْ يَـعْـلَـمَ أَنَّـهُ مَـا انْـتَـقَـمَ أَحَـدٌ قَطُّ لِـنَـفْـسِـهِ
إِلَّا أَوْرَثَـهُ ذَلِكَ ذُلًّا يَـجِـدُهُ فِي نَـفْـسِـهِ ، فَـإِذَا عَـفَـا أَعَـزَّهُ
اللهُ تَـعَـالَى ، وَ هَـذَا مِـمَّـا أَخْـبَـرَ بِـهِ الـصَّـادِقُ
الْـمَـصْـدُوقُ صَـلَّى اللهُ عَـلَـيْـهِ وَ سَـلَّـمَ حَيْـثُ يَـقُـولُ :
((مَـا زَادَ اللهُ عَـبْـداً بِـعَـفْـوٍ إِلَّا عِـزًّا)) .

فَـالْـعِـزُّ الْـحَـاصِـلُ لَـهُ بِـالْـعَـفْـوِ أَحَبُّ إِلَيْـهِ وَ أَنْـفَـعُ لَـهُ
مِـنَ الْـعِـزِّ الْـحَـاصِـلِ لَـهُ بِـالْإِنْـتِـقَـامِ، فَـإِنَّ هَـذَا عِـزٌّ فِي
الـظَّـاهِـرِ وَ هُـوَ يُـورِثُ فِي الْـبَـاطِنِ ذُلًّا ، وَ الْـعَـفْـوُ ذُلٌّ
فِي الْـبَـاطِنِ وَ هُـوَ يُـورِثُ الْـعِـزَّ بَـاطِنًـا وَ ظَـاهِـرًا .

The fifth matter is that it should be known that no one has ever sought revenge for himself before except that he would feel humiliation within himself. If he were to pardon, Allāh would honor him. This matter is from the things

that the truthful and trusted one (ﷺ) informed us of where he said, "The more forgiving the person is, the more honor Allāh shall bestow upon him."

So the honor that he achieves by pardoning is more beloved and beneficial to him than the honor that he would achieve by taking revenge. Verily this honor (achieved by taking revenge) is outward while he inherits humiliation inwardly. Yet pardoning brings humility inwardly while inheriting honor inwardly and outwardly.

Explanatory notes

This statement of the author (رحمه الله) mentioned as an explanation to the Hadīth **"The more forgiving the person is, the more honor Allāh shall bestow upon him."** [2] is tremendous.

So whoever contemplates on the reality of peoples' actions in this regard he will discover that many people think that honor only comes by taking

---

[2] Muslim reported it (#2588) from the Hadīth of Abū Hurayrah (رضي الله عنه).

retaliation or revenge; while withholding to do so is a
kind of humiliation! How can he do such and such and
not seek revenge?! That is humiliation!

Many people think that honor lies in taking retaliation
for themselves whereas the true honor is in pardoning:

مَا زَادَ اللهُ عَبْدًا بِعَفْوٍ إِلَّا عِزًّا

**"The more forgiving the person is, the more
honor Allāh shall bestow upon him."**

Take a look at this beautiful illustration from Shaykh-
ul Islām where he said,

**"So the honor that he achieves by pardoning is more
beloved and beneficial to him than the honor that he
would achieve by taking revenge. Verily this honor
is outward** — meaning, taking revenge only achieves
outward honor.

**While he inherits humiliation inwardly. Yet
pardoning brings humiliation inwardly** — it is
assumed that one who pardons is humiliated — **while
in reality he inherits honor inwardly and outwardly."**

THE SIXTH MATTER

Shaykh-ul Islām Ibn Taymīyah (رَحِمَهُ ٱللَّهُ) said,

السَّادِسُ - وَ هِيَ مِنْ أَعْظَمِ الْفَوَائِدِ -: أَنْ يَشْهَدَ أَنَّ الْجَزَاءَ مِنْ جِنْسِ الْعَمَلِ ، وَ أَنَّهُ نَفْسُهُ ظَالِمٌ مُذْنِبٌ ، وَ أَنَّ مَنْ عَفَا عَنِ النَّاسِ عَفَا اللهُ عَنْهُ ، وَ مَنْ غَفَرَ لَهُمْ غَفَرَ اللهُ لَهُ .

فَإِذَا شَهِدَ أَنَّ عَفْوَهُ عَنْهُمْ وَ صَفْحَهُ وَ إِحْسَانَهُ مَعَ إِسَاءَتِهِمْ إِلَيْهِ سَبَبٌ لِأَنْ يَجْزِيَهُ اللهُ كَذَلِكَ مِنْ جِنْسِ عَمَلِهِ فَيَعْفُو عَنْهُ وَ يَصْفَحُ وَ يُحْسِنُ إِلَيْهِ عَلَى ذُنُوبِهِ ، وَ يَسْهُلُ عَلَيْهِ عَفْوُهُ وَ صَبْرُهُ ، وَ يَكْفِي الْعَاقِلَ هَذِهِ الْفَائِدَةُ .

"The sixth matter—which is among the greatest benefits—is that one recognizes what he reaps what he sows and that he is a wrongdoer who sins; and that whoever pardons people Allāh

will pardon him and whoever forgives them
(i.e., the people) Allāh will forgive him.

So when one knows that forgiving and
overlooking people's harm against him is
means for Allāh rewarding him on account of
the kind of deed he does. So one pardons,
forgives, and treats others excellent despite his
sins; and it becomes easy for him to pardon
others and have patience. This benefit suffices
the intelligent person."

Explanatory notes

Meaning, among the matters that aid the servant in
enduring people's harm, is that knowing that he reaps
what he sows. So if you pardon the people, Allāh will
pardon you for your sins and neglectfulness of Allāh's
(سُبْحَانَهُوَتَعَالَى) rights over you. He will pardon you due to
your forgiving attitude, and Allāh loves those who
pardon people. So when you pardon His servants for
their harm towards you seeking what is with Allāh of
reward, He will reward you based on the type of deed
you have done and He (سُبْحَانَهُوَتَعَالَى) will pardon you.

THE SEVENTH MATTER

Shaykh-ul Islām Ibn Taymīyah (رحمه الله) said,

السَّابِعُ : أَنْ يَعْلَمَ أَنَّهُ إِذَا اشْتَغَلَتْ نَفْسُهُ
بِالْإِنْتِقَامِ وَ طَلَبِ الْمُقَابَلَةِ؛ ضَاعَ عَلَيْهِ زَمَانُهُ وَ
تَفَرَّقَ عَلَيْهِ قَلْبُهُ، وَ فَاتَهُ مِنْ مَصَالِحِهِ مَا لَا
يُمْكِنُ اسْتِدْرَاكُهُ، وَ لَعَلَّ هَذَا أَعْظَم عَلَيْهِ مِنَ
الْمُصِيبَةِ الَّتِي نَالَتْهُ مِنْ جِهَتِهِمْ، فَإِذَا عَفَا وَ
صَفَحَ فَرَغَ قَلْبُهُ وَ جِسْمُهُ لِمَصَالِحِهِ الَّتِي هِيَ
أَهَمُّ عِنْدَهُ مِنَ الْإِنْتِقَامِ .

"The seventh matter is that one should know that if he occupies himself with revenge, he will waste his time, and his heart will become disunited; he will miss out on that which is beneficial to him, and it will not be possible for him to repair it. Perhaps this is greater than the affliction that affected him from the people. But if he pardons and forgives them his heart and body find resolve in that which is beneficial to him more importantly than seeking revenge."

Explanatory notes

This statement from the author is also an important observation pertaining to this matter; that if the person became preoccupied with revenge and started to seek out retaliation then this in reality is a waste of time; and it will cause him to lose a portion of his life which are more beneficial to him religiously or worldly than these matters which he has become occupied with.

So for this reason, it is appropriate for the person to remain calm and say to himself, "**instead of me wasting my time and efforts in the harm (that occurred to me) I will pardon them for Allāh's face (سُبْحَانَهُ وَتَعَالَى) or be patient with this harm seeking what is with Allāh (of a reward) and preserve my time.**"

Hence, having patience with the people's harm is an avenue towards saving one's time and not wasting it.

THE EIGHTH MATTER

Shaykh-ul Islām Ibn Taymīyah (رَحِمَهُٱللَّهُ) said,

الثَّامِنُ : أَنَّ انْتِقَامَهُ وَاسْتِيفَاءَهُ وَانْتِصَارَهُ لِنَفْسِهِ

وَانْتِصَارَهُ لَهَا ؛ فَإِنَّ رَسُولَ الله صَلَّى اللهُ عَلَيْهِ وَ

سَلَّمَ مَا انْتَقَمَ لِنَفْسِهِ قَطُّ ، فَإِذَا كَانَ هَذَا خَيْرَ

خَلْقِ الله وَ أَكْرَمَهُمْ عَلَى الله لَمْ يَنْتَقِمْ لِنَفْسِهِ ،

مَعَ أَنَّ أَذَاهُ أَذَى الله ، وَ يَتَعَلَّقُ بِهِ حُقُوقُ الدِّينِ ، وَ

نَفْسُهُ أَشْرَفُ الْأَنْفُسِ وَ أَزْكَاهَا وَ أَبَرُّهَا وَ أَبْعَدُهَا

مِنْ كُلِّ خُلُقٍ مَذْمُومٍ ، وَ أَحَقُّهَا بِكُلِّ خُلُقٍ

جَمِيلٍ ، وَ مَعَ هَذَا فَلَمْ يَكُنْ يَنْتَقِمُ لَهَا ،

فَكَيْفَ يَنْتَقِمُ أَحَدُنَا لِنَفْسِهِ الَّتِي هُوَ أَعْلَمُ بِهَا

وَ بِمَا فِيهَا مِنَ الشُّرُورِ وَ الْعُيُوبِ ، بَلِ الرَّجُلُ

الْعَارِفُ لَا تُسَاوِي نَفْسُهُ عِنْدَهُ أَنْ يَنْتَقِمَ لَهَا ، وَ

لَا قَدَرَ لَهَا عِنْدَهُ يُوجِبُ عَلَيْهِ انْتِصَارَهُ لَهَا .

"The eighth matter is that one seeking vengeance, full retribution, and revenge for himself[3]; for indeed the Messenger of Allāh (ﷺ) never sought revenge for himself. So if this is the case with the best of Allāh's creation and most honored before Allāh, who didn't seek revenge, and in spite of that him being harmed is an annoyance to Allāh and what is related to the religion. He, himself (i.e., the Prophet Muhammad) is the most dignified, purest, truthful, and one who is void of any dispraised characteristics. He is the most deserving of every beautiful moral. And in spite of this, he did not seek revenge for himself, so how can anyone of us seek revenge for oneself while knowing his own faults and shortcomings fully. Actually, a wise person is certain that oneself is not worthy enough to seek vengeance or satisfy its needs of retaliation."

Explanatory notes

---

[3] **Translator's note:** the original Arabic text here does not have the completion of this sentence.

Meaning, the person should study the biography of the Prophet (عَلَيْهِ ٱلصَّلَاةُ وَٱلسَّلَامُ) for indeed Allāh (سُبْحَانَهُ وَتَعَالَى) made him a role model for His servants just as Allāh (سُبْحَانَهُ وَتَعَالَى) says,

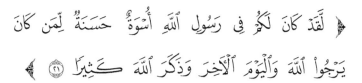

﴿ لَّقَدْ كَانَ لَكُمْ فِى رَسُولِ ٱللَّهِ أُسْوَةٌ حَسَنَةٌ لِّمَن كَانَ يَرْجُوا۟ ٱللَّهَ وَٱلْيَوْمَ ٱلْءَاخِرَ وَذَكَرَ ٱللَّهَ كَثِيرًا ۝ ﴾

"Indeed in the Messenger of Allāh (Muhammad صَلَّى ٱللَّهُ عَلَيْهِ وَسَلَّمَ) you have a good example to follow for him who hopes in (the Meeting with) Allāh and the Last Day and remembers Allāh much." [*Sūrah al-Ahzāb* 33:21]

Indeed, the Prophet's (صَلَّى ٱللَّهُ عَلَيْهِ وَسَلَّمَ) soul is the most honored, righteous, good natured and most elevated in status; and the Prophet (صَلَّى ٱللَّهُ عَلَيْهِ وَسَلَّمَ) never sought revenge for himself and he never became angry for himself (عَلَيْهِ ٱلصَّلَاةُ وَٱلسَّلَامُ) unless the sanctities of Allāh are violated; then indeed he (عَلَيْهِ ٱلصَّلَاةُ وَٱلسَّلَامُ) became angry.

On the authority of Ā'ishah (رَضِيَ ٱللَّهُ عَنْهَا) said,

مَا انْتَقَمَ رَسُولُ الله صَلَّى اللهُ عَلَيْهِ وَ سَلَّمَ لِنَفْسِهِ
فِي شَيْءٍ يُؤْتَى إِلَيْهِ حَتَّى يُنْتَهَكَ مِنْ حُرُمَاتِ الله
، فَيَنْتَقِمَ لله .

"Allāh's Messenger (ﷺ) never took revenge for his own self in any matter presented to him till Allāh's limits were exceeded, in which case he would take revenge for Allāh's sake."[4]

So His biography is impeccably clean of any personal vendetta against anybody (ﷺ) despite the fact that he was gravely harmed on numerous occasions; nor is it transmitted in his brilliant biography (ﷺ) that he sought revenge for himself ever.

Therefore, among the matters which will aid you in enduring people's harm is that you should look in this brilliant biography of our noble Prophet (عَلَيْهِ ٱلصَّلَاةُ وَٱلسَّلَامُ) and you should strive with yourself to follow and emulate his guidance (عَلَيْهِ ٱلصَّلَاةُ وَٱلسَّلَامُ).

---

[4] Al-Bukhārī reported it (6853) and this is his wording; Muslim also reported it (2327).

THE NINTH MATTER

Shaykh-ul Islām Ibn Taymīyah (رَحِمَهُٱللَّهُ) said,

التَّاسِعُ : إِنْ أُوذِيَ عَلَى مَا فَعَلَهُ لله أَوْ عَلَى مَا أُمِرَ
بِهِ مِنْ طَاعَتِهِ وَ نُهِيَ عَنْهُ مِنْ مَعْصِيَتِهِ : وَجَبَ
عَلَيْهِ الصَّبْرُ وَ لَمْ يَكُنْ لَهُ الْإِنْتِقَامُ ، فَإِنَّهُ قَدْ
أُوذِيَ فِي الله فَأَجْرُهُ عَلَى الله .

وَ لِهَذَا لَمَّا كَانَ الْمُجَاهِدُونَ فِي سَبِيلِ الله ذَهَبَتْ
دِمَاؤُهُمْ وَ أَمْوَالُهُمْ فِي الله لَمْ تَكُنْ مَضْمُونَةً ، فَإِنَّ
اللهَ اشْتَرَى مِنْهُمْ أَنْفُسَهُمْ وَ أَمْوَالَهُمْ ، فَالثَّمَنُ
عَلَى الله لَا عَلَى الْخَلْقِ ، فَمَنْ طَلَبَ الثَّمَنَ
مِنْهُمْ لَمْ يَكُنْ لَهُ عَلَى الله ثَمَنٌ ، فَإِنَّهُ مَنْ كَانَ
فِي الله تَلَفَهُ كَانَ عَلَى الله خَلَفُهُ .

وَ إِنْ كَانَ قَدْ أُوذِيَ عَلَى مُصِيبَةٍ فَلْيَرْجِعْ بِاللَّوْمِ عَلَى نَفْسِهِ وَ يَكُونُ فِي لَوْمِهِ لَهَا شُغْلٌ عَنْ لَوْمِهِ لِمَنْ آذَاهُ.

وَ إِنْ كَانَ قَدْ أُوذِيَ عَلَى حَظٍّ فَلْيُوَطِّنْ نَفْسَهُ عَلَى الصَّبْرِ، فَإِنَّ نَيْلَ الْحُظُوظِ دُونَهُ أَمَرُّ أَمَرُّ مِنَ الصَّبْرِ، فَمَنْ لَمْ يَصْبِرْ عَلَى حَرِّ الْهَوَاجِرِ وَ الْأَمْطَارِ وَ الثُّلُوجِ وَ مَشَقَّةِ الْأَسْفَارِ وَ لُصُوصِ الطَّرِيقِ، وَ إِلَّا فَلَا حَاجَةَ لَهُ فِي الْمَتَاجِرَةِ.

وَ هَذَا أَمْرٌ مَعْلُومٌ عِنْدَ النَّاسِ أَنَّ مَنْ صَدَقَ فِي طَلَبِ شَيْءٍ مِنَ الْأَشْيَاءِ بُذِّلَ مِنَ الصَّبْرِ فِي تَحْصِيلِهِ بِقَدَرِ صِدْقِهِ فِي طَلَبِهِ.

The ninth matter is that if one is harmed because of what he done solely for Allāh or because he complied with the commands and refrained from the prohibitions, he is obliged to have patience and not to seek revenge; because

THE NINTH MATTER

he was harmed in the path of Allāh, so his reward will be given by Allāh.

For this reason, when Mujāhidīn's blood and wealth were lost in the path of Allāh as those things were not guaranteed. Allāh, therefore, brought their selves and wealth, so the price is for Allāh to give back not for the creation.

Hence, whoever seeks his price (i.e., retribution) from those who harmed him will not be given his reward from Allāh. Whoever is damaged in the path of Allāh (i.e., seeking Allāh's face) then Allāh will give him a due reward.

If the case is that he was harmed due to an affliction then he should place the blame on himself; and by doing so, this will distract him from blaming the one who harmed him.

If the case is that he was harmed because of a personal gain then he should adjust himself to having patience; indeed, attaining his share involves something bitter than patience. So whoever does not have patience with the midday heat, rain, snow, difficulty of traveling, highway robbers, then he has no need for getting into business.

This matter is well-known amongst the people that whoever is sincere in a purpose, he shall commit to patience as much as his level of sincerity.

Explanatory notes

The harm caused by the people takes several forms:

The first type: is either their harm to him may be on part of something associated with the religion, as in commanding good or prohibiting evil; or calling to Allāh's religion or teaching people good; and so the people harm him because he commanded the good, or he prohibited evil, or he called to Allāh's religion. So he shouldn't seek revenge against them. Rather, he should set his sight on what reward is with Allāh; because this is in the path of Allāh and a harm which occurred while being obedient to Allāh. So he should seek a reward with Allāh (سُبْحَانَهُوَتَعَالَى) and endure their harm because it is in the path of Allāh — He should hope for a reward from Allāh (سُبْحَانَهُوَتَعَالَى).

The second type: is if he is harmed because of an affliction, then he should place the blame on himself —

and in doing so, it will distract him from blaming the one who harmed him.

The third type: is if he were harmed over a worldly matter then he should adjust himself in enduring the harm similar to how people who do business, profiteering, those who seek an earning adjust themselves to harm that occurs in what is expected and hoped for in gains and profit. So the believer is more entitled to have that patience.

46 | P a g e

THE TENTH MATTER

Shaykh-ul Islām Ibn Taymīyah (رَحِمَهُ ٱللَّهُ) said,

الْعَاشِرُ : أَنْ يَشْهَدَ مَعِيَّةَ الله مَعَهُ إِذَا صَبَرَ ، وَ مَحَبَّةَ الله لَهُ إِذَا صَبَرَ ، وَ رِضَاهُ، وَ مَنْ كَانَ اللهُ مَعَهُ دَفَعَ عَنْهُ أَنْوَاعَ الْأَذَى وَ الْمَضَرَّاتِ مَا لَا يَدْفَعُهُ عَنْهُ أَحَدٌ مِنْ خَلْقِهِ .

قَالَ تَعَالَى: ﴿وَٱصۡبِرُوٓاْ إِنَّ ٱللَّهَ مَعَ ٱلصَّٰبِرِينَ ﴾ ۝

وَ قَالَ تَعَالَى: ﴿ وَٱللَّهُ يُحِبُّ ٱلصَّٰبِرِينَ ﴾ ۝

The tenth matter is that one should recognize Allāh being with him whenever he observes patience; he also observes Allāh's love and pleasure for him when he has patience.

Whomever Allāh is with will be protected from harm and damage that no one from Allāh's creation can protect.

Allāh (سُبْحَانَهُ وَتَعَالَى) says,

"And be patient Surely, Allāh is with those who are *as-Sābirīn* (the patient ones, etc.)." [*Sūrah al-Anfāl* 8:46]

And Allāh (سُبْحَانَهُوَتَعَالَى) says,

"And Allāh loves *as-Sābirīn* (the patient ones, etc.)." [*Sūrah Aali Imrān* 3:146]

Explanatory notes

Meaning, one should consider this reward as well as Allāh being with him, and His Love (سُبْحَانَهُوَتَعَالَى) to those who have patience. So this consideration will distract him from seeking revenge, and he will become patient with the people's harm, which results in him becoming among those whom Allāh (عَزَّوَجَلَّ) loves,

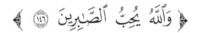

"And Allāh loves as-Sābirūn (the patient ones, etc.)." [*Sūrah Aali Imrān* 3:146]

Also, they will be rewarded with Allāh's company,

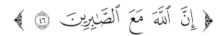

"Surely, Allāh is with those who are as-Sābirīn (the patient ones, etc.)." [*Sūrah al-Anfāl* 8:46]

This form of Allāh being with him is exclusive, and Allāh's aid, protection, success, direction to the right way, support, good, and blessing are obtained. So one should adjust himself to having patience in order to become successful to achieve Allāh's company and His Love.

THE ELEVENTH MATTER

Shaykh-ul Islām Ibn Taymīyah (رَحِمَهُ ٱللَّهُ) said,

الْحَادِي عَشَرَ : أَنْ يَشْهَدَ أَنَّ الصَّبَرَ نِصْفُ الْإِيمَانِ
، فَلَا يَبْذُلُ مِنْ إِيمَانِهِ جُزْءًا فِي نُصْرَةِ نَفْسِهِ ،
فَإِذَا صَبَرَ فَقَدْ أَحْرَزَ إِيمَانَهُ وَ صَانَهُ مِنَ النَّقْصِ
، وَ اللهُ يَدْفَعُ عَنِ الَّذِينَ آمَنُوا .

The eleventh matter is that one should recognize that patience is half of Imān (i.e., true Islāmic Faith). One should not sacrifice a portion of his Imān to seek revenge for himself. Rather, when he is patient his Imān will preserve his Imān and protect it from deficiency, and Allāh will protect those who believe.

Explanatory notes

This, as well, is among the matters that aid with having patience. Patience is half of Imān; and it is split into two parts; one being patient and the other being gratitude. Just as the Prophet (صَلَّى ٱللَّهُ عَلَيْهِ وَسَلَّمَ) said,

عَـجَبًا لِأَمْرِ الْمُؤْمِنِ ، إِنَّ أَمْرَهُ كُلَّهُ خَيْرٌ ، وَ لَيْسَ
ذَاكَ لِأَحَدٍ إِلَّا لِلْمُؤْمِنِ ؛ إِنْ أَصَابَتْهُ سَرَّاءُ شَكَرَ
فَكَـانَ خَيْـراً لَـهُ ، وَ إِنْ أَصَابَتْهُ ضَرَّاءُ صَبَرَ فَكَـانَ
خَيْراً لَـهُ .

"Astonishing is the affair of the believer.
Indeed, all of his circumstances are good;
however, this is not the case for anyone except
the believer. If he is bestowed with happiness,
he shows gratitude, and this is good for him. If
he suffers bad times and he is patient, then this
is better for him." [5]

Hence, Imān consists of Patience and Gratitude. Both
cornerstones are mentioned in numerous verses.

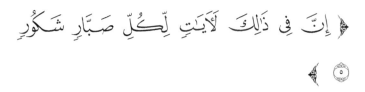

"Truly, therein are evidences, proofs, and signs
for every patient, thankful (person)." [*Sūrah*

---

[5] Muslim reported it (2999) from the Hadīth of Suhayb ar-Rūmī
(رَضِيَاللَّهُعَنْهُ).

Ibrahim 14:5, *Sūrah Luqmān* 31:31, *Sūrah Saba* 34:19, *Sūrah ash-Shura* 42:33]

Both are mentioned in numerous verses; four places in the Qur'ān, hence, the religion and Imān has two halves:

1. One-half is patience.

2. And the other half is gratitude.

So one who was harmed should say, **"I will not seek revenge, rather I will be patient so that I can preserve this great status and high rank in the religion which is patience. Therefore, I will not sacrifice any of it, a small portion, an insignificant amount so that I won't miss out on any of my portion and share of this status that is half of Imān."**

THE TWELFTH MATTER

Shaykh-ul Islām Ibn Taymīyah (رَحِمَهُ ٱللَّهُ) said,

الثَّانِي عَشَرَ : أَنْ يَشْهَدَ أَنَّ صَبْرَهُ حِكَمٌ مِنْهُ عَلَى نَفْسِهِ، وَ قَهْرٌ لَهَا، وَ غَلَبَةٌ لَهَا ، فَمَتَى كَانَتِ النَّفْسُ مَقْهُورَةً مَعَهُ مَغْلُوبَةً لَمْ تَطْمَعْ فِي اسْتِرْقَاقِهِ وَ أَسْرِهِ وَ إِلْقَائِهِ فِي الْمَهَالِكِ، وَ مَتَى كَانَ مُطِيعًا لَهَا سَامِعًا مِنْهَا مَقْهُورًا مَعَهَا لَمْ تَزَلْ بِهِ حَتَّى تُهْلِكَهُ، أَوْ تَتَدَارَكَهُ رَحْمَةٌ مِنْ رَبِّهِ ، فَلَوْ لَمْ يَكُنْ فِي الصَّبْرِ إِلَّا قَهْرُهُ لِنَفْسِهِ وَ لِشَيْطَانِهِ ؛ فَحِينَئِذٍ يَظْهَرُ سُلْطَانُ الْقَلْبِ وَ تَثْبُتُ جُنُودُهُ وَ يَفْرَحُ وَ يَقْوَى وَ يَطْرُدُ الْعَدُوَّ عَنْهُ.

The twelfth matter is that one recognizes that his patience is a form of controlling and conquering oneself. So once one subdues his soul, it won't desire to enslave him and put him

under its captivity, or cast him into ruin. However, once one is obedient to his soul, listens to it, and is conquered (by it), it will carry on until it destroys him or he (survives) it by a descending mercy from His Lord. So if patience has no benefit save subduing his soul and his Shaytān; then at this moment, the heart's power manifests, his soldiers become firm, he rejoices and becomes strong and drives out the enemy.

Explanatory notes

This statement also is among the helpful guidelines in enduring people's harm; that you are patient with their harm, it is a form of gaining victory over one's soul and total control over it in contrast to seeking revenge. For indeed, one yields in front of what his soul demands; which involves gratification and revenge.

THE THIRTEENTH MATTER

Shaykh-ul Islām Ibn Taymīyah (رَحِمَهُٱللَّهُ) said,

الثَّالِثُ عَشَرَ : أَنْ يَعْلَمَ أَنَّهُ إِنْ صَبَرَ فَاللهُ نَاصِرُهُ وَ لَا بُدَّ،

فَاللهُ وَكِيلُ مَنْ صَبَرَ، وَ أَحَالَ ظَالِمَهُ عَلَى الله ، وَ مَنِ

انْتَصَرَ لِنَفْسِهِ وَكَلَهُ اللهُ إِلَى نَفْسِهِ فَكَانَ هُوَ النَّاصِرُ لَهَا

فَأَيْنَ مَنْ نَاصَرَهُ اللهُ خَيْرُ النَّاصِرِينَ إِلَى مَنْ نَاصِرُهُ نَفْسُهُ

أَعْجَزَ النَّاصِرِينَ وَ أَضْعَفَهُ ؟!

The thirteenth matter is that one knows if he is patient, Allāh will defend him and that is inevitable. Allāh, al-Wakīl (i.e., protector) of the one who is patient. He turns over his oppressor to Allāh; On the other hand, whoever seeks revenge for himself, Allāh will leave him to manage his affairs and that he will be the one who aids himself. So consider (the end) of whom Allāh, the best of supporters, supports in comparison to who (chose) to be supported by his soul, the most unable and weakest of supporters.

Explanatory notes

It means: the servant entrusts his whole affairs to Allāh in addition to seeking support, right, and all life affairs from Allāh alone. In the meantime, he commits to patience and awaits the reward of support and success from Allāh (سُبْحَانَهُوَتَعَالَىٰ) for his patience. In the Hadīth,

وَأَنَّ الـنَّـصْـرَ مَـعَ الـصَّـبْـرِ

"And aid come with patience."[6]

---

[6] Ahmad reported it (2800) from the Hadīth of ibn 'Abbās (رَضِيَاللَّهُعَنْهُ) and it was authenticated Shaykh al-Albānī in the book as-Silsilah as-Saheehah (2382).

THE FOURTEENTH MATTER

Shaykh-ul Islām Ibn Taymīyah (رَحِمَهُٱللَّهُ) said,

الرَّابِعُ عَشَرَ : أَنَّ صَبَرَهُ عَلَى مَنْ أَذَاهُ وَاحْتِمَالَهُ يُوجِبُ رَجُوعَ خَصْمِهِ عَنْ ظُلْمِهِ وَ نَدَامَتَهُ، وَاعْتِذَارَهُ، وَ لَوْمَ النَّاسِ لَهُ ، فَيَعُودُ بَعْدَ إِيذَائِهِ لَهُ مُسْتَحِيِيًا مِنْهُ نَادِمًا عَلَى مَا فَعَلَهُ، بَلْ يَصِيرُ مُوَالِيًا لَهُ .

وَ هَذَا مَعْنَى قَوْلِهِ تَعَالَى : ﴿ اُدْفَعْ بِالَّتِي هِيَ أَحْسَنُ فَإِذَا الَّذِى بَيْنَكَ وَبَيْنَهُ عَدَاوَةٌ كَأَنَّهُ وَلِيٌّ حَمِيمٌ ۝ وَمَا يُلَقَّهَا إِلَّا الَّذِينَ صَبَرُوا وَمَا يُلَقَّهَا إِلَّا ذُو حَظٍّ عَظِيمٍ ۝ ﴾

The fourteenth matter is that his patience with the one who harmed him tacitly forces his oppressor, to cease oppression, to regret, and to apologize not to mentioned the people's blame.

So the oppressor will be shy and regretful over his abhorrent actions, and even becomes an ally of the oppressed.

This is the meaning of Allāh's statement:

"The good deed and the evil deed cannot be equal. Repel (the evil) with one that is better (i.e. Allāh ordered the faithful believers to be patient at the time of anger, and to excuse those who treat them badly), then verily! He, between whom and you there was enmity, (will become) as though he was a close friend. But none is granted it (the above quality) except those who are patient, and none is granted it except the owner of the great portion (of the happiness in the Hereafter i.e. Paradise and this world of a high moral character)." [*Sūrah Fussilāt* 41:34-35]

Explanatory notes

This matter which the author (رَحِمَهُ ٱللَّهُ) cited is a matter many people notice with those who tolerate people's harm and meet harm with endurance. So when a person harms you, and you tolerate it, and then he harms you again, and you tolerate it, and he does it again, and you tolerate it and be gentle with him and repel it with goodness. At the end of the matter, the other person will feel shy towards you and apologize to you. His treatment towards you will be in the most delightful manner, and this is the reason it was obligatory to treat him with kindness resulting in you feeling ease. So partake in rectifying the character and morals of others.

THE FIFTEENTH MATTER

Shaykh-ul Islām Ibn Taymīyah (رَحِمَهُٱللَّهُ) said,

الْخَامِسُ عَشَرَ : رُبَّمَا كَانَ انْتِقَامُهُ وَ مُقَابَلَتُهُ

سَبَبًا لِزِيَادَةِ شَرِّ خَصْمِهِ وَ قُوَّةِ نَفْسِهِ وَ فِكْرَتِهِ

فِي أَنْوَاعِ الْأَذَى الَّتِي يُوصِلُهَا إِلَيْهِ كَمَا هُوَ

الْمَشَاهِدُ، فَإِذَا صَبَرَ وَ عَفَا أَمِنَ مِنْ هَذَا الضَّرِرِ

، وَ الْعَاقِلُ لَا يَخْتَارُ أَعْظَمَ الضَّرَرَيْنِ بِدَفْعِ

أَدْنَاهُمَا ، وَ كَمْ قَدْ جُلِبَ الْإِنْتِقَامُ وَ الْمُقَابَلَةُ

مِنْ شَرٍّ عَجَزَ صَاحِبُهُ عَنْ دَفْعِهِ، وَ كَمْ قَدْ ذَهَبَتْ

نُفُوس وَ رِئَاسَاتٌ وَ أَمْوَالٌ لَوْ عَفَا الْمَظْلُومُ

لَبَقِيَتْ عَلَيْهِ .

The fifteenth matter is that perhaps one's seeking revenge and retaliation will be a cause for increasing evil on part of the antagonist and causes him to think of various ways to inflict harm, as it is the common case. So if the one who has been harmed is patient and pardons he will be safe from this harm.

The rational person would not choose the greater of two harms by repelling, the lesser of them. How many times that seeking revenge and retaliation brings about an evil that which the person who seeks it couldn't repel; and how many times the loss of lives, positions of authority, and wealth could have been prevented had the person being wronged only pardoned the other.

Explanatory notes

Meaning, the one seeking revenge from who harmed him may increase transgressor's evil, get worse, and possibly bring an evil that he (i.e., one seeking revenge) has no power over. Hence, enduring the harm is a form of repelling a greater harm. Since the person seeking revenge from his oppressor may empower him to do more evil and bring forth matters which the oppressed doesn't have any power to stand against. So his repelling with kindness and excellent treatment is a means for safety from a more severe harm.

THE SIXTEENTH MATTER

Shaykh-ul Islām Ibn Taymīyah (رَحِمَهُٱللَّهُ) said,

السَّادِسُ عَشَرَ : أَنَّ مَنِ اعْتَادَ الْانْتِقَامَ وَ لَمْ يَصْبِرْ
لَا بُدَّ أَنْ يَقَعَ فِي الظُّلْمِ ، فَإِنَّ النَّفْسَ لَا تَقْتَصِرُ
عَلَى قَدَرِ الْعَدْلِ الْوَاجِبِ لَهَا لَا عِلْمًا وَ لَا إِرَادَةً ،
وَ رُبَّمَا عَجَزت عَنِ الْاقْتِصَارِ عَلَى قَدَرِ الْحَقِّ ،
فَإِنَّ الْغَضَبَ يَخْرُجُ بِصَاحِبِهِ إِلَى حَدٍّ لَا يَعْقِلُ
مَا يَقُولُ وَ يَفْعَلُ ، فَبَيْنَمَا هُوَ مَظْلُومٌ يَنْتَظِرُ
النَّصرَ وَ الْعِزَّ إِذْ انْقَلَبَ ظَالِمًا يَنْتَظِرُ الْمَقْتَ
وَ الْعُقُوبَةَ .

The sixteenth matter is that one who makes it a habit of seeking revenge and become impatient will inevitably fall into oppression. Indeed, the soul is unable to remain within the boundaries of its rightful justice; because of its lack of knowing those boundaries and inability to curb vengeance once it unleashes it; for anger takes the person to limits in which he doesn't comprehend what he says and does. So at this moment, he was a person who was wronged waiting for assistance and honor but now he has changed into an oppressor who is waiting for Allāh's anger and punishment.

Explanatory notes

Meaning, that patience is safer for you and keeps you free of any blame. Because if you pursue revenge and retaliation equally as Allāh (سُبْحَانَهُوَتَعَالَ) says,

$$\text{﴿ وَإِنْ عَاقَبْتُمْ فَعَاقِبُواْ بِمِثْلِ مَا عُوقِبْتُم بِهِۦ ﴾}$$

"And if you punish (your enemy, O you believers in the Oneness of Allāh), then punish them with the like of that with which you were afflicted." [Sūrah an-Nahl 16:126]

Perhaps you will go beyond even by a little of what is equal to the harm (i.e., you were afflicted with). So because of this, you now have been exposed yourself to sin and wrongdoing; and Allāh does not love wrongdoers.

THE SIXTEENTH MATTER

Who has the ability to weigh his retaliation with exact precision where he won't exceed beyond the harm he was afflicted with?!

Hence, patience is the safest measure and keeps him free of any blame with respect to what patience has of great virtues that have been previously mentioned.

THE SEVENTEENTH MATTER

Shaykh-ul Islām Ibn Taymīyah (رَحِمَهُٱللَّهُ) said,

السَّابِعُ عَشَرَ: أَنَّ هَذِهِ الْمَظْلَمَةَ الَّتِي ظُلِمَهَا هِيَ سَبَبٌ إِمَّا لِتَكْفِيرِ سَيِّئَتِهِ أَوْ رَفْعِ دَرَجَتِهِ ، فَإِذَا انْتَقَمَ وَ لَمْ يَصْبِرْ لَمْ تَكُنْ مُكَفِّرَةً لِسَيِّئَتِهِ وَ لَا رَافِعَةً لِدَرَجَتِهِ.

The seventeenth matter is that this act of wrongdoing that one is afflicted with is a means for his minor sins to be forgiven or to raise him in status. However, if he seeks revenge and remains impatient, then this (i.e., wrongdoing against him) will not be an expiation for his sins nor will it raise him in status.

Explanatory notes

Meaning, this act of patience is required in order for the expiation of minor sins and being raised in status. Hence, if he seeks revenge, he will lose out on this great matter of his minor sins being forgiven and being raised in status.

66 | P a g e

THE EIGHTEENTH MATTER

Shaykh-ul Islām Ibn Taymīyah (رَحِمَهُ ٱللَّهُ) said,

الثَّامِنُ عَشَرَ : أَنَّ عَفْوَهُ وَ صَبْرَهُ مِنْ أَكْبَرِ الْجُنْدِ

لَهُ عَلَى خَصمِهِ ؛ فَإِنَّ مَنْ صَبَرَ وَ عَفَا كَانَ صَبْرُهُ

وَ عَفْوهُ مُوجِبًا لِذُلِّ عَدُوِّهِ وَ خَوْفِهِ وَ خَشْيَتِهِ مِنْهُ

وَ مِنَ النَّاسِ ، فَإِنَّ النَّاسَ لَا يَسْكُتُونَ عَنْ خَصمِهِ

وَ إِنْ سَكَتَ هُوَ ، فَإِذَا انْتَقَمَ زَالَ ذَلِكَ كُلُّهُ .

وَ لِهَذَا تَجِدُ كَثِيرًا مِنَ النَّاسِ إِذَا شَتَمَ غَيْرَهُ أَوْ

آذَاهُ يُحِبُّ أَنْ يَسْتَوْفِيَ مِنْهُ ، فَإِذَا قَابَلَهُ اسْتَرَاحَ وَ

أَلْقَى عَنْهُ ثِقلاً كَانَ يَجِدُهُ.

The eighteenth matter is that one's pardoning and patience are among the greatest soldiers that one has against his antagonist. Indeed,

whoever has patience and pardons others will necessitate that his enemy is humiliated; also, his enemy will fear him and the people. For surely the people will not remain silent against one's antagonism even if he remains silent. So if one seeks revenge all of this will cease.

For this reason, there are many people who will feel ease and be more comfortable if the person whom they wronged exacted vengeance against them.

Explanatory notes

Meaning, if you pardon others and are patient, then this will support you against your antagonist. For indeed, one's patience and pardoning will necessitate that his enemy is humiliated, that he fears him (i.e., the person being harmed), and that he has a fear of him and the people. Indeed, the people will not remain silent against him; and in this situation, they will become his defense, his protection, and his supporter without him seeking that from them. This is obtained through his patience, forbearance, and pardoning. So the antagonist will suffer humiliation through harming you, and will cause you to gain aiders and supporters from the people as well as a soldier that Allāh

(سُبْحَانَهُوَتَعَالَ) has mobilized for you in your defense and an obstruction for those who harm you.

THE NINETEENTH MATTER

Shaykh-ul Islām Ibn Taymīyah (رَحِمَهُ ٱللَّهُ) said,

التَّاسِعُ عَشَرَ: أَنَّهُ إِذَا عَفَا عَنْ خَصِمِهِ اسْتَشْعَرَتْ نَفْسُ خَصِمِهِ أَنَّهُ فَوْقَهُ وَ أَنَّهُ قَدْ رَبِحَ عَلَيْهِ، فَلَا يَزَالُ يَرَى نَفْسَهُ دُونَهُ، وَ كَفَى بِهَذَا فَضْلاً وَ شَرَفاً لِلْعَفْوِ.

The nineteenth matter is that when one pardons his antagonist, the same antagonist will realize that he (i.e., the one being wronged) is superior to him and that he has gained something from him. So the antagonist is stuck with perceiving himself inferior to the one he wronged, and this will suffice as a virtue and honor for pardoning.

Explanatory notes

Pardoning is enough as a virtue and honor and the one who pardons the people in return for their harm, they

will start to realize that he is superior to them and
higher than them. Because this, in reality, is honor and
loftiness as previously mentioned in the Hadīth of the
Prophet (ﷺ),

مَا زَادَ اللهُ عَبْدًا بِعَفْوٍ إِلَّا عِزًّا

**"The more forgiving the person is, the more
honor Allāh shall bestow upon him."**

Hence, this is most beneficial for the servant and
greater for his status and standing than him seeking
revenge from the one who harmed him.

THE TWENTIETH MATTER

Shaykh-ul Islām Ibn Taymīyah (رَحِمَهُٱللَّٰه) said,

الْعِشْرُونَ : أَنَّهُ إِذَا عَفَا وَ صَفَحَ كَانَتْ هَذِهِ حَسَنَةً ، فَتُوَلِّدُ لَهُ حَسَنَةً أُخْرَى ، وَ تِلْكَ الْأُخْرَى تُوَلِّدُ لَهُ أُخْرَى ، وَ هَلُمَّ جَرًّا ، فَلَا تَزَالُ حَسَنَاتُهُ فِي مَزِيدٍ ، فَإِنَّ مِنْ ثَوَابِ الْحَسَنَةِ الْحَسَنَةَ ، كَمَا أَنَّ مِنْ عِقَابِ السَّيِّئَةِ السَّيِّئَةَ بَعْدَهَا .

وَ رُبَّمَا كَانَ هَذَا سَبَبًا لِنَجَاتِهِ وَ سَعَادَتِهِ الْأَبَدِيَّةِ ، فَإِذَا انْتَقَمَ وَانْتَصَرَ زَالَ ذَلِكَ .

"The twentieth matter is that when one pardons others and overlooks (mistakes), this is a good deed; that will give birth to another good deed for him. So that good deed will give birth to another and so on. His good deeds will not stop increasing. Indeed, the reward for a good deed is another; likewise, the punishment for a bad deed is another one after it.

Perhaps this will be a means for his salvation and everlasting happiness; yet if he seeks revenge and retaliation that will cease.

Explanatory notes

Meaning, that pardoning and overlooking are counted as good deeds. The reward for the good deed is another one after it, and when a good deed is present, it calls a similar good deed. Hence, the good deeds band together and increase gradually for the servant. However, if he takes revenge for himself, he will lose out on these steadily increasing and consecutive good deeds.

At any rate, these tremendous observations and beneficial guidelines that the diligent Imām, Shaykh-ul Islām Ibn Taymīyah (رَحِمَهُٱللَّهُ) cited will aid the servant in enduring people's harm. He also mentioned great concepts and precious observations which are befitting for every Muslim to ponder over and benefit by them in order to be an aid—by Allāh's permission—in developing this type of patience and actualizing this tremendous status.

May Allāh reward this Imām with the best of rewards for this sincere advice and illustration. We ask Allāh, the Most-Generous, to cause all of us to benefit from what we have learned and increase us in knowledge; and may He rectify all of our affairs and not leave us to handle our affairs for the blink of an eye.

IN CLOSING

I advise you with two matters:

Firstly, it concerns every single one of us that we repeat the study of these twenty guidelines which he (رَحِمَهُ ٱللَّهُ) has cited. Contemplate over the earlier twenty guidelines with deliberateness and good comprehension so you will gain control over yourself and penetrate deep in your heart; and this will become helpful — by Allāh's permission — in having this type of patience and one will call to mind these matters at times of harm and these beautiful concepts will manifest that the author (رَحِمَهُ ٱللَّهُ) had cited by Allāh's leave.

Secondly, is that we should desire to spread these great benefits and we should use the various means of propagating it through electronic means (i.e., the internet, email, etc.) as well as paper (i.e., newspapers, pamphlets, articles, etc.). Indeed, the one who directs towards good is like the one who does it as our Noble Prophet (صَلَّى ٱللَّهُ عَلَيْهِ وَسَلَّمَ) said[7]. Also, complying with the above instructions will be our contribution to limit the

---

[7] Muslim reported it (1893) from the Hadīth of Abū Mas'ūd al-Ansārī (رَضِيَ ٱللَّهُ عَنْهُ).

increasing evil and enmity among Muslims. And Allāh is the only One, who guides to success.

I conclude with the supplications that the author (رَحِمَهُ ٱللَّه) often concluded with. I ask Allāh, the Great, to guide the rest of our brothers and us to His upright path. The path that Allāh has bestowed upon them from the Prophets, the truthful, the martyrs, and the righteous and how excellent are they as companions. Allāh (Alone) is Sufficient for us, and He is the Best Disposer of affairs (for us). May Allāh bless our Prophet Muhammad, his family, and companions and send abundant peace on them.

POINTS OF BENEFIT

POINTS OF BENEFIT

POINTS OF BENEFIT

POINTS OF BENEFIT